TAKE A BOW, B.C.

by JOHNNY HART

A FAWCETT GOLD MEDAL BOOK
Fawcett Publications, Inc., Greenwich, Conn.

FAWCETT GOLD MEDAL BOOKS

in the B. C. series by Johnny Hart

TAKE A BOW, B. C.

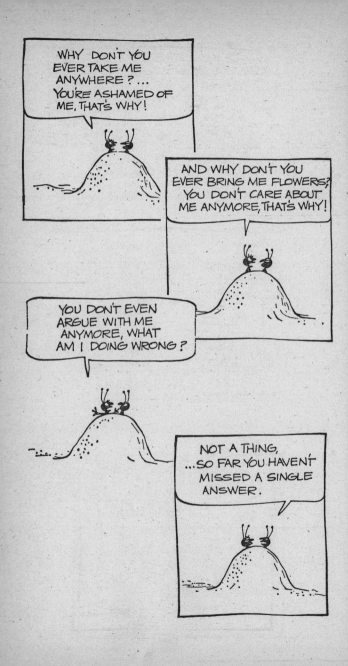

RING

IF YOU CAN GUESS THE NAME OF THE UNKNOWN SOLDIER, YOU WIN 40 FREE DANCE LESSONS.

CRANSTON SNORD.

THAT IS CORRECT.

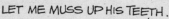

GOLLY,.. HE'S EVEN ADORABLE WHEN HE'S ALL BEAT UP AND DISHEVELED.

FOR A MINUTE THERE I THOUGHT SHE WAS PUTTING ME ON.

WHUMP

GRONK

GROG

GLOOMP

RIP

GROG

BIMP

BEEP
BEEP

YOU'RE UNDER ARREST AGAIN, BOOBY.

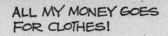

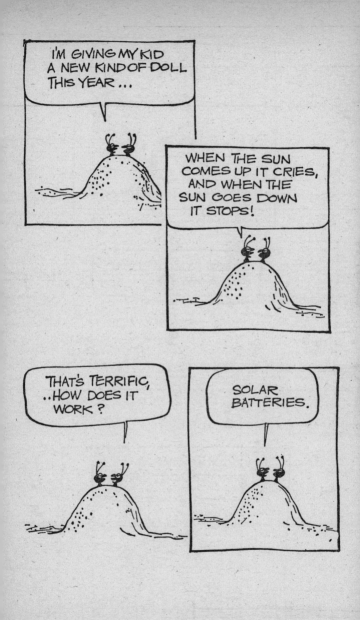

ZOT

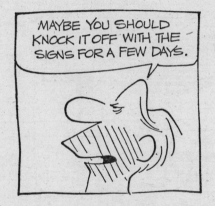

SEE SPOT CHASE BIRDS.

SPOT IS RAPIDLY
STARVING TO DEATH.

LOOK, LOOK.
SEE PUFF PLAY
WITH THE BALL.

SEE THE BALL UNWIND.

SEE MOMMY STAB PUFF
WITH THE KNITTING NEEDLE.

SEE DICK BUY TOYS AND GAMES.

SEE JANE BUY DOLLS AND RECORDS.

SEE DICK AND JANE SPEND MONEY.

DICK AND JANE ARE GOVERNING OUR ECONOMY.

SEE DICK THROW
STONES.

SEE JANE THROW
STONES.

IT IS FUN TO
JANE AND DICK.

BUT NOT TO
THE EMBASSY
PEOPLE.

SEE DICK TAKE THE TEST.
SEE JANE TAKE THE TEST.

SEE DICK COPY JANE'S
PAPER,
SEE THE TEACHER CATCH
DICK.

SEE DICK CLEANING
THE LATRINE.

LOOK, LOOK. SEE THE DETERGENT COMMERCIAL.

OH, SEE THE FILTHY, FILTHY CLOTHES.

SEE THE WOMAN WINCE WITH DISGUST!

SHE IS WATCHING THE DETERGENT COMMERCIAL.

ONE GOOD SHOT
WITH THE TONGUE
SHOULD DISLODGE
THIS LOUSY CLAM.

ZANG

CLAMP

HOW CAN YOU AFFORD TO CUT YOUR WORMS IN HALF?

IT'S EASY, ... I'M SELLING THEM AT HALF PRICE.

YOU'RE ON REPORT, CLUMSY, I'LL GIVE YOU TILL TOMORROW TO FILTHY THIS PLACE UP.

WHO WAS THAT?

THE STATE BAIT INSPECTOR.